# GRANNY NORBAG
## and the Intergalactic Games

By:

Art a

A CIP record of this book is available from the British Library.
First printed 2019 by B&B Press (Parkgate) Ltd, Aldwarke Rd, Parkgate, Rotherham S62 6DY.

www.grannynorbag.co.uk

ISBN 978 1 9993216 2 8

Other GRANNY NORBAG titles available:

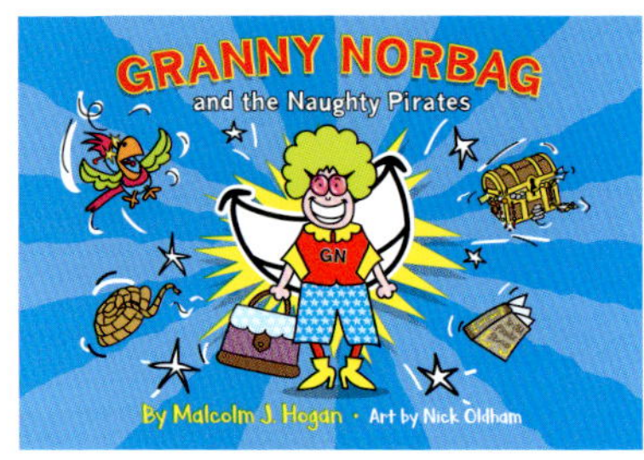


GRANNY NORBAG
AND THE NAUGHTY PIRATES

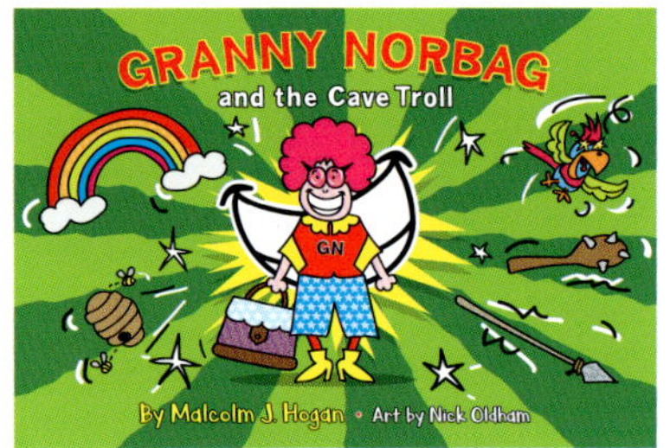


GRANNY NORBAG
AND THE CAVE TROLL

Dedicated to Tyler, Huntressa's biggest fan!

One sunny morning, as she was hanging out her washing, Granny Norbag heard the sound of many rumbling footsteps racing up the hill.

Cheering the runners on
as they passed by, Granny Norbag turned to
Engelbert and said,
"I wish I could compete for a gold medal."

The magic teeth began to chatter and the old lady found herself saying the magic words....
"I wish upon these MAGIC DENTURES for a truly amazing adventure!"
Suddenly, an enormous gust of wind blew Granny Norbag and Engelbert high up into the sky!

In an instant, the pensioner and her feathered friend found themselves looking out at a strange lunar landscape.

"Come with me Granny Norbag!" bellowed a pea-green alien. "You have been selected to represent your planet in the Intergalactic Games."

Realising where she was, an excited Granny Norbag shouted, “Engelbert!! I do believe I’m the first GRAN ON THE MOON!”

To celebrate her achievement, she made a flag from a pair of her bloomers and posed for a photograph.

A short while later, Granny Norbag lined up for the first event.
She felt very tiny stood next to the giant aliens from galaxies far and wide.
EVENT 1
GRRR..
GN
H
H
X

Gurrugg, a menacing creature, tried to scare Granny Norbag before the egg and spoon race began. However, she soon felt better when Huntressa, a tall leopard-like alien, welcomed her warmly and wished her good luck.
I ALWAYS WIN!
GRRR..
EVENT 1
GOOD LUCK!
GN
H
H

Once the race had started Granny Norbag showed the others how fast she was by sprinting to the finish. The crowd celebrated when it was announced that her time was a new INTERGALACTIC RECORD!
EGG & SPOON RACE
1...GRANNY NORBAG
2... HUNTRESSA
3... GURRUGG
GRRR..
GN
H
H

Gurrugg was furious. He had never lost a race before.
"I'm going to finish the day eating a gran sandwich!" he snapped.
BY 'ECK!
GRRR..
GN

Event two was the hammer throw. As Granny Norbag didn't have a hammer she was allowed to throw her heavy handbag instead. "It's the heaviest object in the Universe!" shouted a baffled alien.

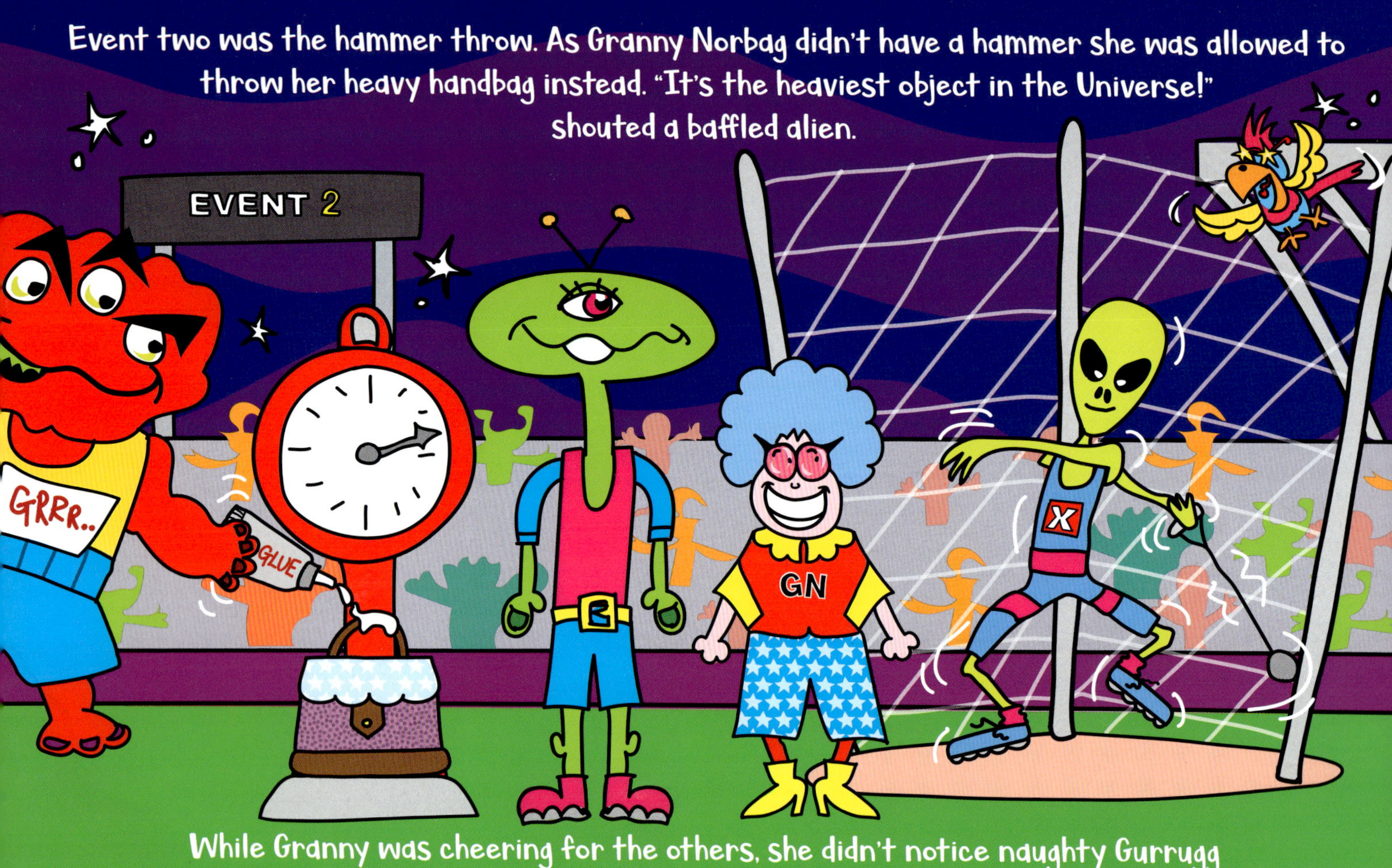


While Granny was cheering for the others, she didn't notice naughty Gurrugg putting some sticky space glue on the handles of her bag.

"Round and around I go!" Granny Norbag chanted as she prepared to launch her handbag. She threw it with all of her might, but she couldn't let go and was soon flying through the air. Everyone looked on in shock except for Gurrugg, who chuckled quietly to himself.

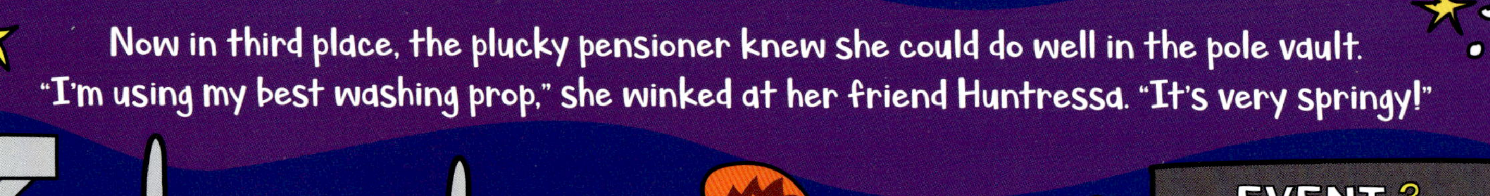

As Engelbert gave Granny instructions, nobody spotted Gurrugg sneakily heading towards the wooden prop with a saw in his hand.

Running faster than a steam train, Granny Norbag launched herself high into the air. The vault looked perfect until the prop snapped in two and she crashed to the floor.
GN
X
Tee Hee!
Wicked Gurrugg clapped his hands as the crowd gasped.
GRRR.

Dusting herself off,
Granny Norbag plucked a green ribbon from her handbag.
"Ooh I love dancing!" she giggled with a twinkle in her eye.

Ooh...
I feel
giddy!
Disco Bag
SLOW
FAST
The crowd cheered as the sprightly O.A.P.
twirled to her DISCO BAG song as it played
on an old fashioned record player. However, she soon found herself tangled in
her own ribbon when a cheeky red finger turned the music to SUPER FAST speed.

As the other competitors enjoyed one of her picnics, Granny Norbag started to cry. She was in last place. "I feel like I'm letting my planet down," she whispered to Huntressa.

But Granny's face lit up like a shooting star when the next event was announced. It was...

## INTERGALACTIC BINGO!

Skilled Granny Norbag won game after game, marking the numbers so fast that smoke came from her bingo dabber!!

"Bingo is MY GAME!" she beamed. The old woman soon found herself in joint first place with Gurrugg and Huntressa.

Whoever won the final event, the MOON MILE, would win the competition.
Engelbert told a T.V. crew that Granny prepared for the race by ...
POSITIONS
1..GRANNY NORBAG
1..GURRUGG
1..HUNTRESSA
4..ALIEN X
5..BAILZ THE ROBOT
Moon T.V.
Moon T.V.
GN
GN
...having her hair permed,
enjoying afternoon tea and going shopping.

The starting gun fired and the final race began. Granny Norbag did not panic when everyone zoomed past her. Clever Engelbert had reminded her that slow and steady would win the race. One by one she passed the other competitors.
EVENT 6
Go for gold, Granny!
H
GN
GRRR..
On the final lap she was about to overtake Gurrugg and go into the lead, when he tried to trip her up.

However, Gurrugg's trick backfired. The bulky alien tripped over his own foot and crashed to the ground with an almighty thud.
I can win this!
GN
AAAARGH!
GRRR..
With a spring in her step, Granny Norbag knew she was about to win the Intergalactic Games.

Upon hearing a loud sobbing sound, Granny Norbag skidded to a halt. She turned to see Gurrugg holding his injured leg. Tears were streaming from all three of his enormous eyes.
I'll help you!
GN
"Take my hand dear," the kind pensioner said softly. "Let me help you finish the race."

A speedy Huntressa soon caught up with them and, without a second thought, she too helped Gurrugg over the finish line.
GRRR..
GN
H
H

Huntressa, Granny Norbag and Gurrugg jumped for joy when the scoreboard showed they had all won the race. The result was beamed all over the UNIVERSE!!!
GN
GRRR..
3 INTERGALACTIC CHAMPIONS!
Moon T.V.
We have three CHAMPIONS!
Moon T.V.

The three winners were presented with their gold medals and trophies. Their flags flew high in the stadium. "I like working as part of a team," Gurrugg admitted to Granny Norbag. "It feels so much better than cheating."

"Before I leave," Granny Norbag announced. "I want to teach you one of my favourite sports...CRICKET!"

Gurrugg studied a book of sporting rules the old lady had given him. He made a fabulous umpire.

Many hours later, Granny Norbag made preparations to return to Earth and climbed on board her rocket. A smiling Gurrugg promised he would never cheat again.

Engelbert squawked the countdown
as the magic teeth began to...
CHATTER!!!
6
GLUE
Moon T.V.
Flying through space, faster than the speed of sound,
the two friends were soon back in their cosy little bungalow.
Arriving just in time to hear...

...the radio newsreader announcing that scientists had discovered a pair of women's bloomers blowing on the Moon.
GN
"If only they knew the truth!" Granny Norbag chuckled as she admired her shiny gold medal and trophy.
Until next time...

'Bye for now!
See you in
our next
adventure!

In the meantime,
you can see more of what
Granny Norbag and Engelbert
are getting up to at:

 @grannynorbag

 @grannynorbag

 @grannynorbagbooks

YouTube Granny Norbag

www.grannynorbag.co.uk

Join Granny Norbag and Engelbert next time as they go on an undercover rescue mission in...

**...THE SPY WHO POURED TEA!**